Estate Planning For The Single Daddy

A Simple Guide To Understanding The Basics Of Estate Planning

Nick Thomas

Copyright © 2015 Nick Thomas

All rights reserved

No part of this book may be reproduced in any form or by any electronic or mechanical means including information storage and retrieval systems, without permission in writing from the author. The only exception is by a reviewer, who may quote short excepts in a review.

Although the author and publisher have made every effort to ensure that the information in this book was correct at press time, the author and publisher do not assume and hereby disclaim any liability to any party for any loss, damage, or disruption caused by errors or omissions, whether such errors or omissions result from negligence, accident, or any other cause.

Visit my website at www.singledaddydating.com

ISBN-13: 978-1505405699

ISBN-10: 1505405696

JOIN OUR COMMUNITY!

Single Daddy Dating is a growing community of single fathers who look to help each other, not only with dating success but in all areas of their lives too. This includes parenting, career and finances advice.

Join us today and get '**10 Crucial Checklist To Dating Success For Single Fathers**' completely FREE!

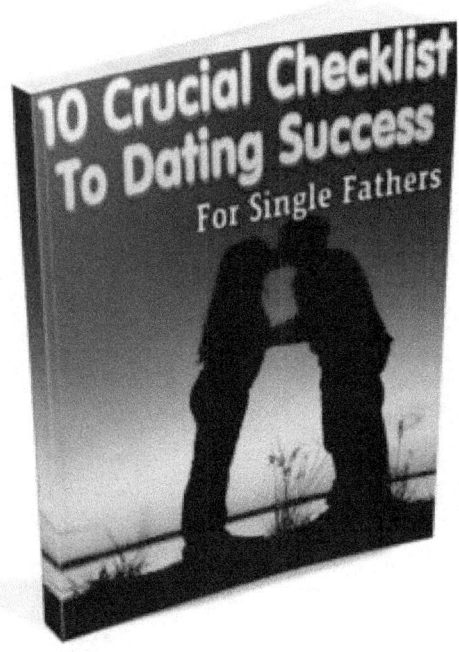

JOIN US AT
WWW.SINGLEDADDYDATING.COM/NEWSLETTER/

NICK THOMAS   www.singledaddydating.com

CONTENTS

Chapter 1: Imagine The Scenario... 1

Chapter 2: The HUGE Benefits OF Estate Planning 5

Chapter 3: Aspects Of Estate Planning 13

Chapter 4: Consideration Before Starting With Estate Planning 17

Chapter 5: Starting Off The Estate Planning Process ... 27

Chapter 6: Costs Of Estate Planning 36

Final Notes 42

Chapter 1: Imagine The Scenario…

Being a single father, I am all about the children. I had three children with my ex-wife, Natalie; and another one (from her previous marriage) with my current wife Helen. Things have been great for me over the years.

As I get older, I am looking to plan for my children's future. I am looking at possibilities in their future that I can help to be a part of. From thinking about their college to their marriage in the future, I am always thinking *"How can I make their lives easier?"*

I already have a college fund for them. My eldest child, Marilyn, would be utilizing the fund that I have for her soon. Other than that, everything is more or less in place. But the one thing that concerns me a lot in the past few years have been understanding the estate planning process.

It's not that I'm rich and have tons of assets. But, I still consider myself fairly well to do, with various properties in my area of residence. I also have a few valuable businesses that have positive cash flow over the years. How do I transfer those assets to my children in the future, if I'm not around?

For me, I am lucky because I trust my ex-wife a lot. However, not everyone is that lucky. Over the years, I have heard of horror stories about the ex-wives from other single fathers. They have shared how these women try to get as much money as possible from them. They simply don't trust their ex-wives.

One thing that I have learned over the years is the importance of having an estate plan. This includes having a:-

- Will
- Living Will
- Health Care Proxy
- Durable Power Of Attorney

All these factors would bring a lot of importance because it saves the hassle of transferring those assets if you are suddenly not around. An estate plan is important especially if you are a single father or divorced.

If you are married and your partner is the biological parent of the child, then it doesn't matter if you have a will. Under the laws of intestacy, your wife would inherit everything automatically. Unless your wife is completely irresponsible, your child would still be taken care of with the inheritance.

If you are a single father, the dynamics change totally. You might not want your ex-wife to inherit your money. Why?

Tell you in the next chapter.

Chapter 2: The HUGE Benefits OF Estate Planning

It is a horrible thing for your ex-wife to inherit your money. But guess what?

Even with divorce papers signed, your ex-wife could still get access to your money, based on the reasoning that she is the guardian of your child. Unless you are okay that your ex-wife with the fact that she becomes the guardian of the child and giving her everything you own, an estate plan is very important. It can be a big danger for you to leave EVERYTHING completely to her if she is known to be irresponsible with money.

That is why having a testamentary trust for the child is important. A testamentary trust is a trust that is created only when you are dead. The assets in this trust would be used for the benefit of your child/children, with a trustee managing the assets based on your wishes.

The appointed trustee would need to manage the funds in a proper way and ensure that it is used solely for the child's best interest. You might also want to leave specific instructions to the trustees. This may include sending them to certain universities and making it a point for the children to visit their grandparents each year.

You can also draft the trust in such a manner that the principal portion of the trust would be distributed to the beneficiary (the child) in a staggered basis, as opposed to a lump sum basis. This is to ensure that the child wouldn't have too much of a money to simply throw around, without having the responsibility or maturity beforehand.

However, control over the money isn't the only problem. There needs to be considerations as to what happens if the other biological parent isn't around or is deceased. That's where having a Will becomes important. A Will would state who would become the guardian of your child.

There are many men who assume that the grandparents would be the automatic guardians in such situations, but there are times where it wouldn't be a good choice. If the grandparents live far away or don't communicate the language, appointing them as guardians wouldn't be a good choice.

Even if you appoint someone as a guardian, the Surrogate Court would need to approve the guardian(s). However, your wishes would carry heavy weight. Unless the guardian has some serious problems such as being an addict or having a criminal record, your wishes would most likely be respected.

There are situations where other relatives may fight for guardian of the child. Some of them have the intention to have a hand on your assets. That is why having a well-planned Will is important. You don't allow other 'relatives' to try to sabotage your wishes by misusing the assets left for your children.

From the following, I hope you understand what I mean by the importance of having a well-thought out estate plan. It can make a tremendous difference in your children's life once you're not around. Among the situations for you to ponder include the following:-

1. **Priority For A Single Father.** Estate planning is an absolute priority for a single father. If your children don't have a

reliable second parent to rely on for their financial support and care, it becomes even more critical for you to take measure to provide for them should you die suddenly.

2. **Incapable Ex-Wife.** In the event of your death, your child's ex-wife may be granted custody. This is in the situation where you are granted custody after the divorce. If you feel that your ex-wife is someone who is totally incapable of being a good parent/guardian, you need to consult your lawyer about this. Talk to him about the potential ways which you can use to mitigate this risk.

3. **Risk Of Selfish Relatives.** Should you die without a will that names a guardian for your children, the court has the power to appoint a guardian and grant custody of your children. It may be someone you don't want or feel that he or she isn't qualified. The court would not know a

person as well as you do. Perhaps you feel a certain relative is completely unqualified to be a guardian for your children. However, if the relative approaches the court and seek custody over your children if he can prove himself. This becomes a risk for you.

4. **Expensive Procedure.** Minor children (below the age of 18) aren't allowed to have ownership of assets beyond a certain amount. If you haven't make detailed estate planning decisions when naming beneficiaries over your assets, the court would appoint a guardian over your estate to oversee the process of inheritance. For such procedures, it would be very expensive. These procedures of getting the property released and approving certain expenditures require the use of a lawyer and would cost a lot. These are all unnecessary expenses that can be saved by having a thorough estate plan. By having

an iron-clad estate plan, you avoid this scenario and ensure money is left to your children.

5. **Power Of Attorney.** Besides having to deal with the event of death, you also need to deal with a situation where you become disabled or incapacitated. If such a situation happens, your children's life would be seriously impacted if you haven't sign a durable power of attorney. A Power Of Attorney gives the rights to make decisions on behalf of you to another person. If you can't communicate, manage finances and pay bills; there would be family members who may go to court to obtain a conservatorship. You never know what they are up to. As such, having a durable power of attorney protects that.

For many of the various considerations, I would explain more about it in the next few chapters. I seriously hope you have given more thought about the estate planning process. You should realize by now how important having an estate plan is.

Without a well thought out estate plan, you would only put your children's life in great jeopardy in the hands of other people.

Chapter 3: Aspects Of Estate Planning

There are various aspects of estate planning. In this chapter, you would learn about the various aspect that you would need to consider when planning your estate.

Will

The will is perhaps the most popular estate planning tool. For most laymen who don't have that much assets, a will helps you transfer your assets upon your death. Having a valid will would ensure that the probate process and the distribution of your assets go smoothly. If you don't have a will, it would be way more difficult. It may take up too much time and end up being very costly.

Besides these factors, you can also name a guardian for your children in the Will. You can also send any messages to your loved ones.

Living Trust

For most people, a Will would be sufficient. However, for some wealthier people, a trust would be more suitable. It is a legal document that becomes valid when you execute the documents and your property is transferred into it.

While you are alive, you manage the assets. When you are dead, it would be passed directly to a trustee of your choice without involving probate.

Although you can't name a guardian for your children in a living trust, you can still use a Will to do so, in conjunction with the living trust.

Power Of Attorney

If you are in a situation where you are incapable of making financial or health-related decisions on your own, a power of attorney allows you to select a person you trust to make them. You would need to tell this person as much as possible and have a Power Of Attorney directive that you have granted them this responsibility.

This is a big responsibility and you would need to choose someone you trust completely. Take time to decide on who should have such tremendous powers on you.

Living Will

This is a document which states your wishes

in certain health-related scenario. While a Power Of Attorney allows another person the decision making power over your care and assets should you be incapacitated, a living will spells our exactly what you want done in specific cases. This may include situations when you are in coma or when you can't be resuscitated.

Chapter 4: Consideration Before Starting With Estate Planning

According to statistics, more than half of Americans don't have a will. A basic will seems so easy to set up yet many people aren't getting it done. Generally, there are two groups of people when it comes to estate planning:-

1. The people who simply don't have their

estate planned

2. The people who want to have their estate planned, but make a mess out of it

If you don't have your estate planned or simply lazy to do it, there is nothing much I can help you. At this point, you can simply stop reading this book and forget about estate planning. I have already tried my best in the previous chapter to explain the importance of estate planning to you.

However, if you fall in the second category of people, I can share with you my experiences about these people. There are many of those people who fall in the second category who tend to make things complicated to a point where it becomes impossible for them to make decisions. More often than not, it is because of information overload.

They become paralyzed by the many considerations they need to make and find it hard to move ahead with the setting up of their estate plan. I have met this couple who were concerned about their estate plans after their best friend suddenly passed away at the ripe age of 39.

They went to learn as much as possible about estate planning to ensure that their two children would be protected should something unfortunate happen to them. They started to overanalyze and had trouble coming up with a suitable candidate for a guardian.

Their parents lived too far away while her siblings weren't suitable. Her brother was deemed to stay too far away as well as in a location that she didn't like. Her sister was a great guardian but had terrible problems with money.

This couple took everything into consideration and simply had the case of "analysis paralysis" – a situation many people have when planning their estates for the first time.

In this chapter, I would share some major questions that you would need to consider when starting off your estate planning. This isn't to make you paralyzed and think too much. Rather, it is main to make you focused about the important questions you need to ask yourself during the process of estate planning.

Question 1: Do you have children who are minors and require a lot of attention?

You may think that you are young and nothing would happen to you now. But you never know what happens. There are many single fathers who are still below the age of 35 and their children haven't even graduate from kindergarten.

Such children requires a lot of attention.

When estate planning you need to consider all circumstances. You may live till you are 90 and see your children have their own children. But, you may be gone tomorrow. Make plans that cover every possibility. Don't worry, you can make changes later as your children get older.

Question 2: Do you have a 'simple' estate?

Is your estate fairly simple and small enough that a single beneficiary can be named on all your assets? If you don't own a home, have less than 5 million dollars' worth in assets and all your assets are highly liquid, then it is alright.

You can easily name a single beneficiary on each of these assets and they will easily bypass probate. You may not need a trust or a will either. However, most estates aren't that simple.

You have other considerations such as the real estate you own, personal items that have great value or other memorable items that mean a lot to your family members. That is another thing you need to consider.

Not everything has a dollar value. Some items may not have much value to other people, but can be highly valuable for your own family members. Therefore, you need to take out a sheet of paper and list down everything that you own and want to give away should you be not around.

Question 3: Do you have a large estate?

Are you someone who has a lot of assets and a high net worth? If you do, you would want to work with an estate planning lawyer. He or she would have to constantly update you about the various changes in the laws. The laws are constantly changing and would impact your tax payable tremendously.

Get advice from them and a tax advisor to see how you can minimize your tax exposure. Besides that, planning your estate well also gives your beneficiaries tremendous tax savings during transfer. You would need to ask your lawyer to explain to you how this happens.

Question 4: Do you have any special demands from the money you leave behind?

If you have a child who is considered 'special-needs', you would like the trust to provide adequately for him. You want to make sure that he has enough money so he can live well.

Besides that, there would also be other wishes that you have with your money. This can be setting aside a sum for a charitable organization or some special people in your life. These 'special people' may not be family members. Rather, they are people who have a big impact on your life and you want to give them some money.

For this to happen, a trust would be more suitable than a will because it has more power to keep on giving when you're not around. For the different wishes you have, you would need to work with a lawyer to set it up. You need someone who is specialized to streamline the entire process.

Question 5: Who should have power of attorney?

A power of attorney is a written authorization to represent or act on another's behalf in private affairs, business or other legal matter; sometimes even against the wishes of the person authorizing the power of attorney (in this case, that's you).

Having a durable power of attorney has great value. During your lifetime, having a durable power of attorney for financial matters allows your representative to manage your funds without being the joint owner of the accounts. When you are setting up your will or trust, the lawyer would have a package that includes setting up your power of attorney.

***

All these questions are important things that you should consider before you start off with the process of estate planning.

It is crucial that you take time to consider there aspects before you even meet a lawyer. You wouldn't want to waste time and money of a lawyer explaining all these considerations to you.

Although there are other considerations that your lawyer may bring up, I have found that these five considerations are the main ones that all single fathers need to consider. You should also understand the various importance of these considerations to ensure you make the right choice.

Chapter 5: Starting Off The Estate Planning Process

In the process of estate planning, it would be advisable to have a lawyer who is an expert in doing it. This is especially when you have a large estate and have complex demands upon them.

Perhaps you want a child to have only a small portion of it and want to give a percentage of your estate to charity each year. Different people have different demands.

There are some parents who have these

'complex demands' to teach their children certain lessons. I have seen situations where fathers choose to have some tests that the child would need to pass before he/she would get his estate. It is not within the confinements of this book to discuss much about this though.

Therefore, hiring a lawyer can help advice you on how to plan your estates better. However, these lawyers are expensive because planning for your estate requires a lot of their time. Added to it your complex demands, it may cost you a bomb to have your estate planned.

I wouldn't say that it wouldn't be worth it, but there are times where there are some things you can do before you start off with the process of estate planning.

Here are some important things to do/consider before you head to a lawyer's office and plan your estate:-

1. Ensure your custody agreements and other court orders are filed with a governing body

Having a formal agreement would help deal with the various problems that would arise when planning your estate. If you don't have a formal agreement, take all necessary steps to get one.

2. List down your assets

The assets that you have include your real estate, savings, insurance plans, stock and bank accounts. You also need to look at your liabilities, which means your debts and other future payment.

As a single father, it would be best if you limit or pay down your consumer debt and mortgage so your estate comprised mainly of income, assets and only taxes liability on your estate once you are death. This will make it much easier for the executor. You would also have a better idea which beneficiary would get what.

3. Decide Your Guardian For Your Children

Who would take care of your children in the event of your death? I have already gone into this consideration in the previous chapter. Analyze the various guardians possible and ask for their permission.

Ideally, you should have two or three choices. Having a back-up matters. What happens if your primary choice dies before you? This is the purpose of a back-up guardian.

When deciding on your guardian for the children, consider the following – do they have good health, are they able handle any financial burdens and able to teach your children well? I look for integrity in a person, because that tells a lot about how they would raise my children.

4. Plan For Other Needs

Your estate would also need to pay for the funeral costs and other tax due upon death, before considering the needs of your family after you have died.

It may seem like a great plan to sell your house to free up cash after you are dead, but you need to consider the tax that arise from the sale. It may not be worth it. It would be better to have your children live in the house instead of selling it.

5. Start An Emergency Fund

This should be an absolute must for every single fathers. This isn't estate planning advice, but plain 'financial' advice.

The extra money can be put aside at the beginning of each month. Make it as automated as possible so you won't be tempted to use it. You can benefit from the compound interest over a period of time.

6. Ensure Your Child's Life Remain The Same

As a single father, I want my children's economic life to remain as unaffected as possible if something happens to me. Things might change if I'm not around, but I want them to have the same standard of living.

You may also want to pay for their education, but bear in mind that there are tons of ways they could fund their own education.

From student loans to grants, the options seem to be endless. The main goal is to provide stability for your children while not burdening the guardian.

You should calculate an estimate of the costs involved to bring up your children until they are 18 if you were to die today. Think about the rental that needs to be paid, the educational costs to put them in school, clothing, entertainment, extracurricular activities etc. It pays to be detailed.

7. Insure Everything

You need to make sure everything is insured, but you don't have to over-insure. This includes having insurance for your mortgage, a life insurance and credit insurance.

All of them are important to ensure your beneficiaries won't be burdened by these liabilities in the future.

8. Meet A Qualified Lawyer

Once you have get everything ready, it is time to meet a qualified lawyer. Ensure that he or she knows all the potential issues that you face together with what you want.

I have seen way too many people go to a lawyer without knowing what they want. It would only waste the lawyer's time, and drive up the lawyer fees.

After you have provided them with all the information together with the possibilities of what you want after you are dead, let them give you their advice. Let your lawyer know who you want to be the guardian, executor and beneficiaries.

Upon your discretion, the lawyer would register your Will with the governing body. This is important because if your lawyer isn't around, there are files on record to show what you intended in the first place.

Among these documents also include your statement of worth, which details your assets and liabilities. It is important to update this statement regularly. You also need to reassess your Will when there are any major life changes. This can happen when you have more children or remarry. Ideally, you should look to assess this situation annually.

9. Have A Back Up

Having your own copy of the documentation would help tremendously. It would help if you get a safety deposit box to store those documents. This gives you proper access to it without risking it from a fire or flood.

***

These few steps can be very helpful for single fathers who have never gave estate planning much thought. Every step has its importance that you need to consider.

Make sure that you have addressed all potential issues that would arise. It would be a real weight off your shoulder, as well as for those who could be affected by your possible early demise.

Chapter 6: Costs Of Estate Planning

I can completely understand why many single fathers neglect their estate planning. For some, money can be so tight that they never think about it at all.

Moreover, estate planning is so expensive if you don't know what to expect. It can be very painful to pay for estate planning as lawyers charge a lot of money. Worst still, you don't even understand the real benefits of it until you are gone.

Why spend money on something when you can't see any immediate benefits?

That becomes a common question many single fathers ask. This is why many single fathers don't have a Will. They simply find no reason to do so. However, there is an argument that doing something cheap is better than not doing anything. This is true. Even a basic Will would save a lot of money for the living, if you pass on.

If you die without a Will (intestate), the state law would decide what to do with most of your belongings. It would not be in a way you want, and would trouble your children. It would cost them plenty of money and pain to get back those assets. Do you want that?

For many single fathers, the do-it-yourself planning seems to be the only way. If your situation is simple, this approach is better. However, you must know that even if you have a simple situation, there are many permutations that could go wrong. These mistakes would end up costing your children a lot more than you saved in legal fees.

But, should you hire a lawyer then?

Even if a lawyer can secure many things, it pays to know that not every Will written by a lawyer would be perfect. Things can still go wrong. This is simply the nature of estate planning. Even lawyers are using software to prepare these documents.

As such, you can easily get an estate plan which is cost-efficient. Below are important estate-planning documents which wouldn't cost too much. Get a legal pro to prepare them and see you can have the lawyer add any other 'add-ons'.

1. **Basic Will.** The basic will is the most important document of estate planning. The purpose is to transfer assets, appoint a guardian for your children (minors) and name an executor. This could be done easily with a software. However, there could be problems because there are certain areas of asset transfer that requires

an experienced lawyer.

2. **Durable Power Of Attorney.** This document appoints a family member, friend or advisor as an agent to act on your behalf. This include several different matters such as financial and legal matters if for some reasons you can't. A good lawyer should be able to help you determine the rules/clauses that apply in the local legislation. There also needs to be a consideration of whether a POA is needed if you own assets are in different states as the rules differ.

3. **Living Will.** Unlike a basic will, this expresses your preference about some aspects of end-of-life care. This is commonly a big debate on euthanasia, whether or not to end a person's life if in a terminal situation.

4. **Health Care Proxy.** This is different from the power given from a living will. This

proxy is authorized to make medical decision on your behalf if you can't. This form isn't difficult to fill out, but it can be difficult to choose someone as your agent due to the high risks involved. Even if you can find someone suitable, he or she may not want to take on such a role.

These four documents aren't the only documents in an estate plan. There are other important documents too. I wouldn't know how to get reasonable cost for all documents. You would need to ask other single fathers about it. I done my research on these four documents and I know that they can be cheap to do if you get the right lawyers.

Many estate planning lawyers can do them. You simply need to ask them to 'add-on'. You would need to negotiate with them. If you want to try other forms of service, you can check it at these resources:-

- **The Estate Planning Source.** This

website offers and intensive network of lawyers in the United States that focuses specifically on living trusts. Although there is a paid membership, signing up for the FREE MEMBERSHIP would also allow you access over an incredible amount of information. Check it out at:

www.singledaddydating.com/EPsource

- **Estate Planning Organizer**. I learned plenty about estate planning from this course. It has plenty of valuable information that anyone serious about estate planning MUST GET. Priced at $197, it may seem pricey. For the information that you get, it is simply peanuts. Check it out at:-

www.singledaddydating.com/EPorganizer

Final Notes

To be frank, getting my estate planned was overwhelming. There were many things to consider and I didn't know how to start. I knew it was important, but at the same time, I knew I would have to do a lot of work.

Even after writing this short book, I wouldn't say that I'm at expert at estate planning. The knowledge that I have is just minimal because I want to help other single fathers understand its importance.

There are some single fathers who are completely unaware about its importance and they become fearful when I tell them about it.

I don't know what prompted you to read this book, but I hope it would give you a basic understanding of estate planning. The purpose of this book isn't too overwhelm you with information. I have purposely written a short book because of this.

Instead, I hope you have understand the importance of estate planning and know how to start planning your estate. You want your children to be protected. Life is very uncertain and you don't want your children to suffer if you're not around.

Once you have considered the various factors in estate planning, then you can start to plan your estate. One great way to start is to get the Estate Planning Organizer. If you are serious about getting your estate planned, this is an essential course. Check it out at:- www.singledaddydating.com/EPorganizer

You may plan to use a professional estate planner and I hope this book helps you gain a basic understanding. You would know what to ask your estate planner and what his duties are.

Having planned your estate, it would give you a good peace of mind. I wish you luck as a single father.

LEAVE A REVIEW

I hope this book has helped you well. It isn't my intention at all to go deep into the topic. I am no expert in everything. However, I have the help of many other single fathers who have shared with me their invaluable experience.

If this book has helped you in any way, do leave me a review. This helps build our single father community.

If you feel that this book can be improved in any way, do mention it in the review. I would love to hear from you.

I wish you luck as a single father…

ABOUT NICK THOMAS

Nicholas Thomas has helped many single fathers cope with divorce in the past few years. By helping them gain more confidence and stability in their lives, he is able to guide them towards being a man that attracts other women easily.

He divorced back in 2008 and knows how difficult a divorce can be for a man. It was a terrible time for him when he got his divorce. He envisioned his children blaming him and not being able to spend time with him. It gave him a constant guilt trip.

Being a divorced man can be very difficult. Ever since his 'emotional recovery' from the divorce, he has helped many single fathers by advising and helping them gain confidence.

Should you want to share your story with him, you can do so at
www.singledaddydating.com/shareastory/

ALSO BY NICK THOMAS

(1) Dating After Divorce For The Single Daddy

(2) Dating Ideas For The Single Daddy

(3) How To Be An Alpha Male

(4) First Date Conversations

(5) Online Dating

(6) How To Approach Women

(7) Mature Dating

(8) Single Parent Support

(9) Coping With Divorce

(10) Parenting After Divorce

Visit www.singledaddydating.com/bookstore/

Get Your Complimentary
FREE BOOK

Join our community today and get **<u>10 Crucial Checklist To Dating Success For Single Fathers</u>** FREE, delivered right to your email…

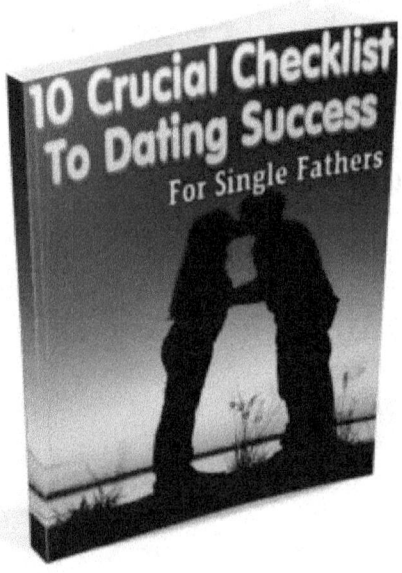

JOIN US AT
WWW.SINGLEDADDYDATING.COM/ NEWSLETTER/

www.ingramcontent.com/pod-product-compliance
Lightning Source LLC
Chambersburg PA
CBHW071819170526
45167CB00003B/1374